BIKINIS AT THE END OF THE WORLD

KELVIN C. BIAS

ARCHIVE ZERO | NEW YORK | 2025
www.archivezero.com

Published by Archive Zero, LLC

E-book ISBN: 978-1-955722-30-8
Paperback ISBN: 978-1-955722-31-5
Hardback ISBN: 978-1-955722-32-2

Copyright © 2025 by Kelvin C. Bias

Cover design by Robson Garcia Jr.
Cover photos: Courtesy of the Library of Congress, LC-DIG-ds-02945 and LC-DIG-ds-02944 (Operation Crossroads at Bikini Atoll in the Marshall Islands, July 1946, taken by the Army Air Forces)
Formatting by Polgarus Studio

Names, characters, places, businesses and incidences either are the product of the author's imagination or used fictitiously, and any resemblance to actual persons, living or dead, businesses, companies, events, or locales is entirely coincidental.

No part of this book may be used or reproduced in any manner without written permission from the author, except in the case of brief quotations embodied in an article or a review.

for swimsuits and global issues...

CONTENTS

Introduction xiii
Lagoon 1
The Legion Of Warm Days 2
The Russian Man In Brooklyn 5
Bolt Out Of The Blue 7
Freeway 8
What Is A Man? 10
I Hurt A Fly 11
Hand 13
Glove 14
Thoughts 15
Prayers 16
Please 17
Respectful 18
The Bomb 19
Future 21
Past 23
Stage 24
Expense 26
Audience 27
Hear 28
See 30
Liquid Insanity 32
Avoid 33
Include 34
Mistake 35

Grit	36
Unbelievable	37
Believable	38
Plead	39
Encounter	40
Basic	41
Address	42
Expect	43
Deny	44
Furious	45
Charge	46
Unlikely	47
Bath	48
Essence	49
Silver Boots	50
Green Bikini	51
Throes	52
She Looked Like You	53
The Commander	55
Seagulls	56
Exhaling	57
Earth-Shattering	58
God Stays	59
The Sighs Of Love	60
Provocative	61
Flavorless	62
The Dead Of July	63
Meuse/Muse	64
Bleeding	66
Lead Ambition To The Kill	68
Zero-Proof	69

Light	70
Dark	71
Relief	72
A Faint Patch Of Blue	73
Hiroshima | Nagasaki	74
See You Yesterday	75
Burn	77
Seven Crows Dream On A Telephone Line While Cars And Buses Belch, Lovers Unplug Their Devices, And Invisible Data Cheats. One Bird Says He's Glad He's Not Human, Not Some Demon Tripped On A Wire, A Player Of Fire, A Prince Among Liars. The Other Six Smile, Then Depart One By One. The Knowing Sky Winks As The Lone Crow Laughs. The Six Return In A Flock—Fooled By The Acrid Air, The Acid Clouds, The Arid Land—And Caw. *Caw, Caw, Caw, Caw, Caw, Caw.* They Are Glad Too, Wasted Food For The Taking Is Easy To Find, Five And Dime. Seven Crows Still Dream On A Telephone Line.	78
The Hallway Of Dreams	79
Sister Wisdom	80
Common	81
Ground	82
Below	83
Above	84
Hibernate	85
Hide	86
The Spell	87
Seek	88
Practical	89
Useful	90
Because	91

Supra Et Ultra.. 92
Winner 94
Ethiopia 95
Priorities 96
Streetwise 97
Sugarman 98
Survivor 99
Frustration 100
Faithful 101
Deceitful 102
Grateful 103
Soulful 104
Walk With Angels 105
Majestic 106
Redemption 107
Humane 108
Numbed 109
I Hope I'm Naked When The Bomb Goes Off 110
Desensitized Plank 111
Sexy Mango 112
Peacock 113
Hoofing It In Brooklyn At 2:02 A.M. 114
27 Million Degrees 115
Black Marrow 116
Beautiful Funeral 117
Old Cars In Black & White 118
Sisyphus 119
Spinoza's God 120
Summer Heat 121
Deterrence 122
Phaethon 123

What Is Memory?	126
The Salt Comes At Unusual Times	127
Trains At 3:39 A.M.	128
Desert Island Movies	129
Advertising	130
Screams Of The Dead	131
The Archaic Ward	132
13%	133
The Dog With One Eye	134
The Big Bangs	135
Cold Drinks	137
Hopeful AI Lie	138
Giant	139
Waking Before The Sun	140
My Heroes Killed Your Heroes	142
Her Name Was Calliope	143
The Power Of No	144
Purpose	145
Vexilla Regis Prodeunt Inferni	146
Rod Serling Narrates A Nuclear War	147
Bikinis At The End Of The World	148
Eden	152
Oboete (覚えて, Remember)	154
Setsuko	156
Nuclear Non-Proliferation Organizations	158
Acknowledgments	161
Other Work By Kelvin C. Bias	163
About The Author	171

"Nuclear powers must avert those confrontations [that] bring an adversary to a choice of either a humiliating retreat or a nuclear war. To adopt that kind of course in the nuclear age would be evidence only of the bankruptcy of our policy—or of a collective death-wish for the world."— President John F. Kennedy in his "A Strategy of Peace" speech at American University on June 10, 1963.

INTRODUCTION

When I was eight, I stared at the sky in front of my suburban Los Angeles home. A blinding flash ripped the sky. I dropped to the ground, flush to the six-inch-high curb near our driveway. I survived. A pocket of non-superheated air saved me. After sitting up, I saw destruction in every direction. I awoke terrified, clutching my chest to see if I was alive. It was a horrible dream. I hope it wasn't a premonition.

The world has been in a precarious position since the detonation of the world's first atomic bomb on July 16, 1945, at the Trinity Site in Alamogordo, New Mexico. Today, there are more than 12,400[1] nuclear warheads in the arsenals of nine (known) nations. Nearly 90 percent of the world's nukes belong to two of them: Russia, run by a dictator, has the most with 5,580, and the United States, helmed by an authoritarian convicted felon, has 5,225. Given the "leadership" in the two most-nuclear-bomb-addicted nations, the world careens in an even more perilous direction.

Compelled to revisit the realm of my childhood nightmare, I wrote a collection of poems primarily about nuclear war—its provenance, its terrifying aftermath, and its potential extinction. A good friend often tells me to stop with the nuclear-bomb talk—to envision a better world—but I have a very hard time doing so given the state of my country and the world. I fear the planet my

---

[1] Source for nuclear warhead figures: Arms Control Association (Jan. 2025 update)

children—all our children—will inherit. I want it to be a verdant Earth, not a world destroyed by human carelessness. These poems are a klaxon. As if we needed another reminder. I must write my conscience. Tonight, when I go to bed, I will dream big—like my grandmother used to say—of a better world with truth, justice, and the *HUMAN* way. In fact, let's all dream peacefully, bigly.

Kelvin C. Bias, New York City

September 2025

BIKINIS AT THE END OF THE WORLD

LAGOON

There abides a place
We'll aspire to be,
Far from the clouds
Of radioactivity,
A new lagoon
Beneath God's ceiling.
Blue trapped in blue:
Multitudes of manufactured fish,
Coconuts with every dish.

But we are not alone
In our surrealist archipelago.
Plastic beat us to the karmic punch.
Soon, we'll shriek and spin,
Rollick in washed up gin,
Eat each other for lunch,
Concoct spits with palm fronds.
Then, we'll understand true bliss.
Paradise is the land with no bombs.

THE LEGION OF WARM DAYS

Sun-soaked skin
Marks the norm.
Everyone, the same[2].
Bronzed feet[3]
Temper the sidewalks,
Dashiki[4] moods,
Bend beneath the
Ultraviolet madness,
From Kentucky to Khartoum,
Planets in disarray.

When the wish for
A tropical ray
Peaks passé,
We'll want the
Black steel of
Chicago's
Winter plight.
We won't want

---

[2] In the not-so-distant future, humans will be a similar shade of brown, what with unchecked climate catastrophe and melanin harvesting centers on dome-protected street corners across the globe; Jesus will still be depicted as white.

[3] The New International Version of the Bible says Jesus' feet "were like bronze glowing in a furnace."

[4] A brightly colored, loose-fitting shirt worn in West Africa. All references were removed from the Smithsonian in 2028 because they weren't "scientifically justified."

The legion of
Warm days.

We'll want ice
In the eternal
Summer haze,
Not Louisiana ICE[5].
We'll want Bomb Pops[6],
Floes on every river.
We'll want what
Hector's[7] selling,
Not branded bibles.
We're beyond hallelujah.

We'll want
Past acreage on
Lake New York[8]'s
January shores.
We'll want
New Antarctic ice[9],

---

[5] U.S. Immigration and Customs Enforcement, not crystal meth.
[6] An extinct brand of ice popsicle with an original red, white, and blue rocket shape that crashed in the 21st century climate collapse.
[7] Not the Trojan prince, a Mexican-American street vendor who was wrongly deported to Mars in 2035.
[8] Emperor Tiny Hands, a cyborg clone, renamed Lake Ontario in the mid 21st century.
[9] Antarctica becomes ice-free by 2075 and corporations divvy up the Southern continent's ice sheet. They sell it to water-starved cities such as Las Vegas, Dubai, Phoenix, Los Angeles, San Diego, Cairo, and MAGA City, a place where bitcoin refugees can drown their sorrows among shredded pieces of a fake Constitution that are touted as authentic.

Nordic[10] flights.
We'll want to
Shield our eyes
From the obsidian[11] sea.

Therein lies racism's epitaph.

---

[10] The tall, white-skinned Nordic aliens believed in some circles to already inhabit the Earth.
[11] A black market—using obsidian as currency—develops after the polar ice caps melt and a new chain of highly-active volcanoes rises in the Atlantic and Indian Oceans.

THE RUSSIAN MAN IN BROOKLYN

The Russian man in Brooklyn
Burned my finger with his key.

Pristine silver, a whimsical phantom,
A duplicate divined for another universe.
Hot off the steel machine,
Whirs, grinds, spins,
Particles of metal voodoo to
Unprotected eyes.

They have weapons too.

July's juniper sun gone nuclear.
People roamed the streets
Happily showing skin.
Brazen, bold, true.
Cancer, be damned.
We have life to live.
Gin, one arm of choice.
Flings another.

They have weapons too.

The Russian man in Brooklyn
Burned my finger with his key.
Go figure, it was
My left middle finger.

I have weapons too.

BOLT OUT OF THE BLUE[12]

Unprovoked? Or a sick joke?
The banners root in fear.
What if every nation had nukes?
Would we act differently?
What if nobody did?
Rocks in slingshots, bolt out of the blue.
War, it's what we do.
Why must humanity skirt the brink?
Shrink from the paste of intelligence?
In no small words: what can be done?
Schrödinger's thermonuclear cat
Exists alive and dead at once.
World, cut to the evolved future
Where peace—borne of reason,
Not destruction—possesses
A pronounced, lasting chance.

---

[12] "Bolt out of the blue" is the U.S. Nuclear Command and Control's name for an unwarned nuclear attack on the United States. Source: *Nuclear War: A Scenario* by Annie Jacobsen (2024)

FREEWAY

Back in the modern
Stone Age—the time
Before everyone had
Warhol's 15-minute whirl—
People read newspapers
Without the "benefit"
Of divisible social media.

One man built a house
In a tree overhanging the
605 Freeway in suburban L.A.,
Next to a miniature golf
Course. They wrote stories
About it, showed it on Channel 7.
A man in a tree: *Film at eleven!*

Another man attached
Balloons to his bed and
Floated away toward the stars,
Above the men with star maps,
And he too received his due.
The freeways looked like snakes
Slithering to their eternal hole.

This man reminisced about
The other men, the other
Childhood dreamers, the other
Fame seekers in their floating
Beds—egos traveled to their
Own distant galaxies far away—
Then he jumped on the freeway.

WHAT IS A MAN?

What is a man?
A tall drink of sand,
A go-go dancer
On a stage in Japan?
He's a pinkie-toe turner,
He's whistled at when
He walks down the street,
He's venomous breaths
Beneath a canopy of lust,
The back alley fears him.

What is a man?
He's not brave,
He cries, he asks
For permission,
He apologizes, he
Cups his hands with
Eyes to the sky's days.
He tends to wounds
With gentleman's gauze.
He has no gaze.

I HURT A FLY

I hurt a fly on
A hot day in July.
Perched on a
Poland Spring,
The horse variety
With its bulging
Red compound eyes.
I killed this fly.
Now will I die?
Yes, yes, I will.
One day, hopefully in
Forty-five more Julys.

My alibi? I quenched thirst
The fly did too.
Resting,
A summer taboo.
I smashed him
With the butt end
Of recycled plastic.
The guts, greenish,
A dash of yellow.
The bug plopped to
The black abyss of the
Refrigerated shelf.

Now no one can say
I wouldn't hurt a fly.
Why did I?
(On the same day,
I saved a morning
Spider trapped in a
Plastic bowl.)
Maybe the fly would
Spread disease,
Regurgitate on a
Slice of pizza pie,
Distract a driver,
Cause an accident?
Wishful thinking,
Absolving guilt.
I just wanted to hydrate,
Not worry about karmic debt
As I guzzled cold fluid.
I exited the bodega,
Walking tall, but
The worst of it all:
After the last drop,
I was still thirsty,
Thinking about that fly.
Will that be every July?

HAND

I am mesmerized
By your blonde sea,
Captivated by
Your hand in mine.
By my hand when
You're no longer around.
These vagabond thoughts
Whisper into a golden morning,
I cannot control myself,
The prospect of dawn's kiss
Spins skyward, hotter
Than a nuclear fire.
This hard notion burns.
We make love while Earth crumbles.
Bodies pressed like diamonds
To make it all go away.

GLOVE

Your white-glove beauty
Hovers at the edge of the vanity,
A clutch of pearls, songs from '68,
Wine stains you don't want
To wash out because they hold
Memories to be relived and exploded.
Rinse and repeat, the dust stays,
Coats us with its dainty dint.
Carpet edges capture nuts and
Other past detritus, heirlooms
Of better times and lost lovers.
Be not afraid in this forensic jag.
In reality, in imagination, in time:
I am your white-glove wizard,
Screaming from the balcony,
I am yours, I am yours, I am yours!

THOUGHTS

I'm naked again,
A spirit in the atomic drafts
Of bygone ecstasy
And airy possibility.
Will you wait for me?
(Equally inscribed
In libidinous rapture.)
Send me more and more.
Signals and blasts
From a faraway saxophone,
A lingering fusion.
Obese comforts fall,
We dance in each other's mind.
We roll over, satiated,
And clench again,
Deeper than friends,
Longer than lovers,
Beasts in time's sea,
Thoughts adrift—
Protagonists of lore.

PRAYERS

Your ear,
Your hair,
Your nails,
Embedded
In my skin.
Send me prayers,
Overtures in the night.
A good dream,
A moonlight encounter,
Ghosts in the distant corners:
I long for them all.
I cross the vestibule of souls,
Marinate in your apocalyptic grace.

PLEASE

Run roughshod
Over the slippery slope
Of remote viewing
And happy to see you,
Sit on the throne of ecstasy,
Rendezvous with audacity,
Rhyme with the smiles
Your body begs.
These pleasant spring
Mornings engage sanity
In the face of destruction.
Please stop the wars.

RESPECTFUL

If I'm respectful,
Nothing happens.
The fall leaves fall,
The winter flakes
Float in silence,
And nuclear fusion has
Unfulfilled dreams.

Audacious, I unfurl
Before you, a renegade
Bathed in your loving sun.
Blonde streaks, hips,
Blue eyes, memories,
Happenstance, and
Green lights disobey.

THE BOMB

I am singular.
I am plural.
I am the mother,
The father of
Every tomb,
The progenitor
Killing future wombs.
I scoff at your
Human hubris.
I am a machine,
I follow orders,
Buttons pushed,
Atoms smushed.
Amiable, I see
Things on high,
I, lord of the sky,
Sea, land, without care.
Why was I built?
To tend to your
Need to weave quilts?
There is no good reason,
A parade of bad actors
(Only one addict has used),
On a world stage, giddy
With the gluttonous
Chance to wield power,

To ferment desolation.
In my final breath, I cry,
Scream into the void:
Exist? Why o' why must I?

FUTURE

Taste the future,
That everlasting
Lollipop, sweet,
Ripe, full—no
Matter how many licks.

Luck ascends,
Planes descend.
Love hovers
Somewhere in the
Middle, dandelion
Dander adrift on air.

The yellow weed
In the field of time
Serves as a lighthouse.

Align 1,000 lights
In a row, and we'll pause
When we see a gap,
A black speck amid
The shine. The hole
Haunts us, but
It's the present.

We assemble 1,000
More lights ahead,
While the past fails.

We continue to
Build, to destroy,
To look back, not
In anger, but in awe.
We are the mouth,
Eating the future
Bit by bit by bit.

PAST

We were naked beasts in heat,
Wedded to the idea of continual pleasure.

We were slippery politicians,
Navigated to the erotic positions.

We were queen and king,
Mitigated by our own deceit.

We were fastidious lovers, discreet,
Elongated in the sheets.

We were discussing a future,
When it happened.

And now we rule the past tense.

STAGE

The lights dim.
There's a show,
But no audience.

We are in the
Blue Room,
Destined to begin.

We spin into
The grins of old,
Lathered in skin.

We make love
To forget the
Tide and times.

We were once
Hatchlings,
Incubated in sin.

Now, the sun
Withers as
We bomb Eden.

We pull the
Curtain over
Our naked bodies.

We are beauty
Personified,
Dreams intact.

Will the lights
Return? Or will we
Burn the stage?

EXPENSE

The skies of winter
Overlook the battlefield.
Live at my expense.

AUDIENCE

I want to make love to you.
Is it wrong of me to ask?
The red towel quenches
Beads of mocking water,
As I spill my desires onto
The white tile floor that
Has seen blood, mucous,
Pus, turquoise toothpaste,
Horrors, insatiable breaths,
Dollops of wayward shampoo.

I want an audience with you.
Is it wrong during other tasks?
The notions of distraction we
Used to discuss in earnest,
Like daffodils bending to the sun,
Suffer for lack of present continuation.
This red towel, the not-so-antiseptic mien,
They are cousins to the toothpaste I
Spit into a residue-stained red plastic cup.
We used to be young too.

HEAR

Here and now.
Hear and how.
The voices
Emanated
Through the wall.
Two lovers coiled,
Unsprung by
Bed springs and
Liquor, perhaps
Something thicker.
Their catcalls,
Louder than
Niagara Falls,
Slid down the
1970s era wood.
Their sighs
Beckoned eaves.
Gaudy green
Carpet shagged
The floor while
The interloper
Loped in his own
Misery, attuned
To the empty room
On the bleak side
Of the emergent sound.

He stood, ear pressed,
Lunged perplexed
In his imagination.
It had been 20 years.
She, of the orange tone,
Rainbow smile, and
Ticklish skin. The
Delicacies of lost
Time remained pinned.
The noisemakers,
Oblivious, as he
Rested his head
On the empty pillow,
Cold like Antarctica,
And went to bed.
He heard the moans
All the way to Bethlehem
In the first night of the war.

SEE

The woman with white hair
Waved the desolate man through
The portal into a world of longing.
He had questions, she
Claimed to have answers.
When he crossed the threshold,
She turned the sign on the door:
Closed. The night bloomed.

She took his coat, black like
Obsidian spit from Iceland.
The cards appeared like spirits:
Death first, portended rebirth.
He wept into her arms, the stench
Of sadness swept them away
In a river of tears that slicked the streets.
They, bound for a different swirl, embraced.

The rest of the deck disappeared, drenched,
The distant clang of the train, the skyscrapers,
The minions of lonely commuters, all bled,
Smeared by the catastrophe of hope.
She, the see, whispered in his ear,
Dulcet notes until they reached the sea.
The moored ships snagged their bliss,
The visionary and the hollow chap drifted.

The duo dated their own dream,
She, the roller coaster, he the rail,
Coney Island at the sea floor, rusted
By time and neglect, while desire rushed
To the sweetest depths, arranged fate.
They held hands, guided by mermaids,
Water, life, the kelp of eternal bonds.
Then, in the axis of peace, they wed in Atlantis.

LIQUID INSANITY

The drops descend,
Children of clouds.
We call it rain.
Birthed by comets,
Life wiggles in water's grace.
Pure, until the lords
Of energy fiddle with destiny,
Use the liquid for their
Rods, in an isotopic
Bed of insanity.
Heavy or light?
Pressure, tight.
We need energy
While moderation flees.

AVOID

Avoid the void.
The sibilant
Darkness
Envelopes
The stars,
Obscures a
Path for
The self-
Assured
Explorer,
Instills cold
Lessons
Miles from
Utopia.
Snarl toward
The brimful
Fecund orbs,
The seas in
Goldilocks' zone.
Pieces of rock
Peal sin away
Amid slivers of
Light, bask in
The feral rawness
Of your modern
Thoughts. We are
Well past simians.

INCLUDE

Remember those
Campfires, the
UFOs in April.
They sting,
Cauterize the eyes,
Float through the
Skies like clouds.
Soon, all will see.
Take me with you.
Include the best me.

MISTAKE

Bitters and buoyant tastes:
These are our tools.
We are not a mistake.

Pleasure is not a mistake.

Self-medication is a process
And we are the lube.

Pleasure fills us with grace.

Tune up, turn the radio down,
We can't hear our exhalations,
Our demonstrative slings
Into the night, groping
For tenderness, compassion,
Understanding, radiance.

Pleasure is not a mistake.

To be made in record time,
We peel ourselves from the floor.
We forget every war.

Pleasure allows us posthaste.

GRIT

The gears of life
Gestate in the
Bottoms, the
Alighieri nightmare,
Burning to be
Set free.

UNBELIEVABLE

The "President" has the
Power to launch a nuclear
Attack even if
Every adviser objects.
No talk of peonies.
Or little girls
Plucking petals.
STRATCOM on Line No. 1.

BELIEVABLE

Nothing he says is believable.

PLEAD

I am baptized
But who is he?
Finger on the button,
Tears as the Dome
Closes its doors,
Tears at the utterance:
"In God We Trust."

E. Pluribus Unum,
Out of many one?
I cry in the wilderness.
I cry in the ocean.
I cry in a divided nation.
I submit my steed.
I don't have a white horse.

ENCOUNTER

I am the watching woods.
Your glistening skin eludes.
I am the snatching thief.
Your beauty transcends.
I am the suitor at the door.
Your mind seeps into mine.
I am your annihilation encounter.
Your body makes peace explore.

BASIC

Summer laughter, friends.
Silence, sex, winter tacos.
Clean air, nourishment.

ADDRESS

Hesitant to call a fire a fire,
The elephant in the room
Stalked the executive proceedings.

Constitution constituting,
A rippled kern on the lake of
Fire, speeches from the ashes.

The flatulent words, the
Disappeared people and
Lands. Damn, man.

There was—but never is—nothing more to say.
Mushroom clouds won't abate.

EXPECT

Where doors weep
In the altogether,
The shadows cling
To the hinges, and
Light commands your
Chambers. I am
The watcher, a servant
Of end all be all
Fantasy. Where
We expect the smooth
Air, leisure, grace.
We wield love to end war.

DENY

The Nile streams year-round.
The abject truth in your
Sphere trickles like a
Drip-drop faucet. Verbiage
Cuts deeper than a dagger.
Deny 'til you die? Perhaps
We're already dead, hiding
Salient facts that reveal
True desires, true freedom.
We must flow from our demons.

FURIOUS

We wallow in the sacraments of apocalypse.

CHARGE

Plug me in.

UNLIKELY

In the unlikely event
We're living ghosts
In a safe aftermath,
We'll pull toward the stars.

Mammoths of time and place,
The shards of love will replace
The shards of destruction.
We'll sympathize with doves.

BATH

People are selling bathwater,
Why not sell a nuclear vacuum?
Or a device to lift your spirits
When the detritus of democracy's
Demise decides to deposit itself
In the deepest part of your domain?

From these weary hands.

Everyone admires beauty.
Let Calgon take us all away.
Uproot the Capitol Dome, dip
It into the muddy Mississippi,
Put it through a global-sized strainer
To filter the strands of secession.

From these weary lands.

We lament the age of division.
Cleanse the nation, go to the beach,
Wear your finest birthday suit.
Don't eat candy, flirt in fitness.
Ditch the Zero bars, bikinis, fast cars.
Let the water flow, avoid the bloodbath.

From these weary stands.

ESSENCE

Gams game,
Pointed to the sky.
Trees, grass,
The insects below
Pay no attention,
For we are joined
As one, in community,
You and I, fluidity.

The sacred sun beams.
The wind whispers
Erotic obscenities.
Cheekbones pierce
The clearing, blood
Pumps unfettered,
Toes shoot toward Venus.
We are vapor.

SILVER BOOTS

She eclipsed everything in the nook,
A work of stark art among art's arch work,
The muse of muses, fallout's last young Turk.

GREEN BIKINI

I'm envious of a piece of thread,
The strings you pull, the affect
Their softness has on me
In this morning haze of summer
When no one infiltrates paradise.

Everywhere we go it's a beach,
Life the curdled tapestry of joy.
Drop your green bikini, flash
The excited sun, the happy sand.
There is only love, be brash.

THROES

Pings and pangs.
Without you I'm done.
No more pleasure,
No more fun. I'll
Hire the sun and
Kiss the moon.
Wish we were in the blue room.
Throw caution in the bin.
You, hot leather,
I, sacred spin.

SHE LOOKED LIKE YOU

She looked like you.

Mouth open on a picnic table,
Sometime in June, they
Call it love in the afternoon.

She looked like you.

Skin bare to the world,
Hand tight to the table,
She beckons thrills.

She looked like you.

The trees filter sunlight
Past a bent red sign,
The green leaves,
The whole nine.

She looked like you.

I stare from afar,
She has your curves,
Your hue, your *je ne sais quoi.*
I want to climb.

She looked like you.

Across the park's lake,
She hides from view,
But I notice the
Swaying hips, the
Engaged lover,
She holds Armageddon
Vagrant in her lair.

She looked like you.

Now I'm sad, for
My melancholy lingers.
The times we spent
Here spring to mind,
Luxuriate, and dine.
I must leave this den.
I must keep my mind sublime.

She looked like you.

THE COMMANDER

He once gazed at the stars,
Navigated by their perilous light.
Attacks at dusk and dawn,
Torpedoes and fate, gambles and dates.
Now he's an artifact, the man at the rail.
He feeds ducks, stares at birds,
Imagines great heights, wallows in
Long-forgotten lows. What with
His eternal question, the plinth of loss:
What would his 90-year-old self do?
What risks? What bold kisses?
Fall through time's cruel grasp.
He is 90, nightingale by this rail.
He laughs when he sees children.
If they only knew, war is not gladness.
The sadness of what might have been,
The twilight destiny of the heavens,
Reeks greater, the true commander.

SEAGULLS

When the black clouds rot,
The smell dissipates, there
Are no tell-tale signs,
The multitudes of lovers
In their burial tombs,
The aftershock of apocalypse,
The plenitudes dry.

But we'll still have the
Ocean birds—they of
The squawking ever-present
Panoply. Follow their scent,
Their distal calls.
They carry the future wind,
Or the sea means nothing at all.

EXHALING

Winter's wayward wrath.
It's five minutes past midnight.
Are we exhaling?

EARTH-SHATTERING

Last fall, I fell hard.
An atomic blast burned bright.
Then, she saw the light.

GOD STAYS

We pray,
God's rays.

We pray,
God's days.

We pray,
God stays.

THE SIGHS OF LOVE

I don't want your apologia.
I want your tender mood,
Your enveloped presence,
The raindrops off the rooftops
When the air rises in June.

Let's rest in the bed of life,
Marinate in the sighs of love
That radiate upon each other.
And from one another.
Reliquaries, we're the sound of relief.

PROVOCATIVE

A brigade of boys blinked when the beauty
Bounded betwixt bohemian blocks in six-inch
Blue heels blaring an atomic blast badge across
The bosom of her cobalt blouse, the
Blueprint for bedlam and blasphemous bends.

FLAVORLESS

Don't tell me there are
No yellow peppers in
The produce section.

Don't tell me the world
Lacks color, integration,
Dances, beautification.

Flavor is the life of spice.
Sex, ice cream, a May day.
We could all use some paprika.

Flavorless factions spread disease.
Jump on the trampoline, sing.
We need everyone's tangerine.

THE DEAD OF JULY

You're on the deck of a yacht, alone.
The black sky, the seer of night,
Watches as you lean against tomorrow.
There are no guardians, no parents,
No pen pals to propel into the dark.

Beautiful colors, flash bangs, booms.
Somewhere on the Mediterranean,
You spot visions of what you want to see.
You seek lovers in the dead of July,
Bowed toward the blinding lights of lust.

MEUSE[13]/MUSE

The stone has not moved in
Millions of years.
That's what they say.
Decay delay,
Delay decay.
Fears are not
Allayed. Naked
Muses cannot
Seal this deal.
A Faustian bargain
Worse than tariffed steel.
Nuclear, nook-lee-air,
Waste, taste, haste.
Rocks made of clay,
Not to rearrange,
To stain, to shun,
To hide the drain,
Deep in a French grave,
Radioactive lies
To bury, to spray.

---

[13] Located 1,600 feet beneath the northeast France district of Meuse, the Meuse/Haute Marne Underground Research Laboratory studies a geological formation of Kimmeridgian claystone as a storehouse for high-level radioactive waste. The facility is run by the *Agence nationale pour la gestion des déchets radioactifs* (ANDRA), and scientists say the rock hasn't moved for several million years.

Allez, allez, allez!
No way, no way, no way.
How much fungi on
Our plate today?

BLEEDING

Where does the blood flow?
Where do idle thoughts go?

My wrists aren't cut,
And don't plan to be,
But I'm always bleeding:
When the sun rises
Between the blinds,
When I get dressed,
When chastised for
My personal style,
When the hot girl
At the coffee shop
Stares deeply into
My melancholy eyes,
When the bed bends
My back in contortionist
Contours, when the sky
Doesn't deliver snow
In the dead of winter,
When people in movies
Engage in amazing sex,
When nothing comes to
Fruition when I press
The flesh, when altitude
Curves my intestines,

When the mundane
Pervades, when
Eternity is much shorter
Than forever and a day,
When I no longer have
The month of May.

Where does the blood flow?
Where do idle thoughts go?

LEAD AMBITION TO THE KILL (Inspired by Akira Kurosawa's *Throne of Blood*, in turn inspired by William Shakespeare's *Macbeth*)

The cawing of crows
In the Forbidden Room.
Arrows of lies,
Arrows of cries,
Arrows of flies
How high does the
Pile of bones
Have to rise?
Through forest, fog,
O'er black sand,
No one escapes the arrows of doom.
A grave for everyone: The End.

ZERO-PROOF

The tempest flaunts no enemies,
She moves wherever she pleases,
Lasts as long as she wants,
Turns men to ash on a whim,
Her song penetrates ambition.
She is the drink without regulation,
Zero-proof zephyr, iron gold, black rain,
The drunk at the bar shattering glass.
Her reputation precedes the need
For explanation, and souls follow.
Year-by-year her howls heighten,
Until ossuaries long for flesh.

LIGHT

Tactile, textile,
My touch is light.
My thoughts are light.
My breath is light.
My body is light.

Patterns, refractions,
The catoms of joy,
The diatoms of diabolical
Design spring free,
Fulgent in the
Symbiotic coast of darkness.
They are light too.

DARK

Prometheus unleashed
Vengeful matter, fire in the night,
Unintended for the droids.
Then we rage-quit gods,
In body, if not mind.
One day we'll return
To the dark.

RELIEF

Malcolm, Martin,
Their physical
Attenuation lies
In clothes, pictures,
Papyrus, files,
Statues, graves,
Memorials, gone
In a Chinese doorway,
A Russian voting booth,
North Korean sincerity,
With the flies of Jan. 6.
Anomaly? Free grief?
In 1,000 years,
America, what is
Your bas-relief?

A FAINT PATCH OF BLUE

You know the feeling of the rolling hills
In the feral night before sun's eye.
The contiguous emptiness, corn and birds lurk.

The ancestors keep watch, multiply as
The terminator approaches—the God of grace.
The clouds delineate life, a faint patch of blue.

Where have we gone? Be it song or drink.
The underground sentinels loom as
The dotted line demarcates the road, a moon departure.

HIROSHIMA   # NAGASAKI

The Dome, the blight   The second city.
Of blights, now a thing   Twisted men,
Of beauty, twisted   The deed makers,
Colorful paper, or one   Twisted women,
Color, blinding white,   The innocent,
Like that terrible light,   Twisted children,
Swans destined for eternity,   Metallic Urakami angels.
Always remembered.   Remember not to forget.

SEE YOU YESTERDAY

The phrase of the future
Resides in the folly of today:
See you yesterday.

BURN

The light through the window,
Accrues energy piercing dust,
While I lay in the aftermath
Of carnal ablation, a singed
Feather—only bones remain.
My flesh oozes off the page of savory
Memories, captured by rapture.
Beads of sweat glisten, soldiers
In a never-ending battle
Against boredom and the mundane.
Fierce cats, we whimper at the notion.
Blinded by heat, we still feel, still
Smoke the residue of love,
That demonstrable arbiter of truth.

SEVEN CROWS DREAM ON A TELEPHONE LINE WHILE CARS AND BUSES BELCH, LOVERS UNPLUG THEIR DEVICES, AND INVISIBLE DATA CHEATS. ONE BIRD SAYS HE'S GLAD HE'S NOT HUMAN, NOT SOME DEMON TRIPPED ON A WIRE, A PLAYER OF FIRE, A PRINCE AMONG LIARS. THE OTHER SIX SMILE, THEN DEPART ONE BY ONE. THE KNOWING SKY WINKS AS THE LONE CROW LAUGHS. THE SIX RETURN IN A FLOCK—FOOLED BY THE ACRID AIR, THE ACID CLOUDS, THE ARID LAND—AND CAW. *CAW, CAW, CAW, CAW, CAW, CAW.* THEY ARE GLAD TOO, WASTED FOOD FOR THE TAKING IS EASY TO FIND, FIVE AND DIME. SEVEN CROWS STILL DREAM ON A TELEPHONE LINE.

Seven crows.

THE HALLWAY OF DREAMS

I run to you, you to me,
But we make no time,
No distance covered.
Suspended, we animate
Our carnal imaginations.

We continue into flight
Notice slight electrical signals.

I am not deterred, nor are you,
For we gallivant in the
Hallway of dreams.
We slowly join hips,
Become glue,
One substance stuck
In a willing dance.

We rebel into the
Folds of time, into the
Forest of abundance,
Into our seas—atoms
Fervent in fusion.

SISTER WISDOM

They've already discussed it more than you know; they clutch the nuclear key.

COMMON

The flash tore the sky into pieces,
Equal to the factions that shadowed the land.
Red, deep, the rain turned frogs neon green.
Everyone held hands, turned to the
Book of Common Prayer—tattered papers.
Kings laughed in wells, turned to demons
Without shells, turned to greed as harmony,
Exiled the non-entities of diversity.

But it was Calvary in a Kansas barn,
The laying on of hands, mistaken grain,
They turned to headless horses to survive,
Blended stark landscapes into pies,
Turned to the eyes of clouds, still turned
Their backs on logic. Science and God,
God and Science—common friends,
Common deeds, common ends.

GROUND

Zero-time flies.
The thoughts,
Desires, futures,
Ground to dust.
We shall rise
From the ashes,
Erect new ideas,
Hew to love,
Scale heights into
Tomorrow's skies.

BELOW

We blow down doors,
Enrich passion instead of
Uranium.
We are the bombs
Burrowed below ground.

ABOVE

So below, so above.
So, suffered against
The mind's walls,
Regaled with blue
Parapets and pertinent
Flags of democracy's grace.
We do not crave conflict.

HIBERNATE

Pierce my winter dreams.
I bask in your dark mercy,
Store food for weeks,
While we feast on
The bounties of
Rhythmic demonstration
In a cave of our choosing.

Pampered by fur,
The showers of emotion
Bind, unblind, by time.
We are immune from
Cataclysm, wet with sleep,
Waiting for spring's gifts,
Omnivores at rest.

HIDE

I cannot hide.
My intentions
Lounge in visibility.
They rise with
The Sun as the
Sun rises with you.

THE SPELL

In the first few seconds,
Millions vaporized.
We played in the woods,
In a soulless Rockies meadow,
Fall day, sun out, clothes off.
We didn't know life as we
Knew it had come to a halt.
We bided in our own heat.
We cast spells,
She on me, I on her.
Breasts and buttocks,
Meat soon to be spoiled.
The leaves just
Starting to turn yellow.
Oblivious, we exploded.
There would be no one to tell.
Naked for our last
Illustrious spell.

SEEK

There's no need to seek.
I will never hide.
Everything is bare,
Easy to find, hard to
The touch, sweet to
Satiate, warm to
Your staunch glare.
In these final hours,
Our radiation peaks,
The missiles launch.

PRACTICAL

The physicist
Studied his books.
Summa cum laude.
Diplomas, paper,
Equations for days.
Society dozed,
Hid in nooks.
Visited the Cape,
Escaped the hate.
Tests and applications.
Blueprints and
Diabolical aspirations.
Build bombs to
Quell the others.
War does end,
But does its necessity?
Ticker-tape lakes,
Deep fakes, deep takes,
The hooks creep.
Meanwhile, we kissed
In Times Square.
We took photos,
For posterity,
Recreate it
When it's gone.
What if the
Physicist studied art?
That's not practical?

USEFUL

If every consenting adult
Around the globe made
Love at the same moment,
The ogres of war might
Not be game anymore.
They won't auger extinction,
But bathe in syncopation:
Jazz, hip-hop, classical.

The flower shops desist
When nuclear weapons
No longer exist,
When the collective
Forces of human ingenuity
Focus on different flora,
Foraging in the wild:
Tulips, lilies, roses.

Lovers of peace
Fornicate in the meadows
Where clean air injects
The global malaise,
Sets an example for
What could be and
Rummages forever in
The attic of useful purpose.

BECAUSE

Because I know she's strange.
Because I know she wants to run off the page.

Her ample legs strangle discussion,
Bleed into nothing, the oblivion
That occurs in deep slumber, like
Manna fallen from the lips of a satiated giant.

We,

Smash,

Ridicule,

Madly.

Because one day we'll decay.
Because subversion keeps depression at bay.
We are not Hollywood, porn, or red stars,
Because our love could start a nuclear war in white heels.

SUPRA ET ULTRA[14]

Godspeed.
I plead.
I can't fathom
The battlefield.
Where are the missiles aimed?
Are there weapons
On distant worlds
Pointed at Earth?
An unknown deterrence,
Furnaces
In a universal oven.

Maybe
The answer
To Fermi's Paradox[15]
Lies in intelligence.
Intelligent creatures.
Love and leave us
Alone
Until

---

[14] The Latin motto of the National Reconnaissance Office (the U.S. government agency overseeing the country's intelligence satellites); it means "Above and Beyond."

[15] The contradiction between the lack of definitive evidence of extraterrestrial life and the high probability that it exists, given the billions of stars in the Milky Way similar to our sun. Physicist Enrico Fermi famously asked: "Where is everybody?"

We evolve
Above nuclear greed,
Beyond
The nuclear need.
Or just
Let us
Destroy
Ourselves.

WINNER

The battlefield
Stomachs silence,
Earth, a garden of
Inaudible cries.
Nobody abstains,
Nobody remains,
Just powdered,
Ash-coated flies.
A wayward cairn
Perpetuates dirt:
We won! We won!
Radiation: the grand prize.

ETHIOPIA

Mountains rise,
Mountains fall.
Sunset sets its
Eyes on every land,
On every sea, every
Dead cemetery. So,
Assemble peacefully.

But lift the trumpets,
Blare the klaxons.
The pulse of disorder
Needs retraction.
Reject dystopia.
Know there are great
Surgeons in Ethiopia.

PRIORITIES

We care more about bikinis than nuclear winter.

STREETWISE

After the bombs went off
There were no streets,
There was no metal oasis.
The clocks disappeared.
But cesium ruled, an irate lover.
We were wise only at the end.

SUGARMAN

They called him Sugarman.
Sweet steppin' since the age of 3.
Tap tap tap, clackety clack clack.
Suit tan, Skin brown, soul Black.
Some people hurled another word
In the direction of his ear, not his feet:
One that began with an "n," not nightbird,
No lie. The girls cried, "Sugarman, Sugarman."
A pawn in a larger game he couldn't see.
He survived the Great War, Harlem Hellcat,
No one cared in the winter snow, so,
He danced a rhyming jig in the Cotton Club.
He danced and danced, much too sweet.
Fedoras and chocolate angels, anvils, tin cans.
The weight of decades fast in his glide.
He danced until he bled, fell, and died.
Known to none, known to Kingdom Come,
His feet kept their checkered shoes.
Long after his demise, he dined with Hughes.
Plaques and signs, rhythm and blues,
The streets, sleek black, with rain-slicked plans,
The wind still whispered his name: Sugar, man.
As he tapped in the Underworld.

SURVIVOR

The country?
The people?
Where have we fled?
The cesium winds blow
Across the land of the dead.
Petri dishes ride.
Fungi, bacteria, viruses.
Which insect takes succession?
Which Latin motto will elide?
Survivors survived by *a* survivor.

FRUSTRATION

Time's aged, my dear.
This spring desert collapses
Each night, on each passage
Of the moon, the tides
Flip at noon, and we…
Still don't act.
We are the king and queen
Of frustration, so let's blow
Our tops without explanation.
Declare a truce, elation.

FAITHFUL

Can we stay in this universe
A little while longer?
Face-to-face, heads sideways,
Eyes glued to infinity.
This is the old way,
With feelings, touches,
Glances, actual kisses,
Breaths brushed across chests,
Hands clasped in glee,
Body parts in synchronicity,
Dreams in a mouthful.
Why can't we be faithful?

DECEITFUL

The taboo of lies
Waits on the threshold,
A fox nibbling at the door.
The evolution of words,
The exacting smile, the
Glass-eyed alacrity
Born of a few cocktails:
These are the weapons.

The bedroom beckons,
A fountain of yearning,
A kaleidoscope of lust,
Mixed with a dash of Eros.
The walls prepare their
Dishes, cluttering sounds
Of the outside world fade.
Why can't we be deceitful?

GRATEFUL

Your hips,
Bearing fruit,
Your effervescent
Saunters through
The world and
The sentience
You stir in trees,
Your mouth,
Pressed flesh
Flanked in red,
Your food,
The candle of
Romance, and
This apocalyptic
Burning; I am
Grateful.

SOULFUL

I breathe in the world,
Take power from its luster,
Pray in every month.

WALK WITH ANGELS

"Walk with angels. Always smile,"
The Showtime man said to the
Peregrine little girl on the L.
Brooklyn-bound, about town,
She didn't have a dollar in hand.
The show was over, but
The performance just began:
The lives, the fellow passengers,
Our ship, car 8216, we all daydream.
Some glued to their smartphone,
Others, hands on their chin,
As if the universe were a problem
To be solved. This is our sphere,
But there are no answers here.
Except in the words of the man,
Who has a plan and a baseball cap
Brimmed with dirty bills—Andrew Jackson,
No, George Washington, yes.
Meanwhile, the angels,
City harbingers, ride a crest.

MAJESTIC

Will the edge of night
Bring calamitous ruin,
The sting of dry death,
Or the majestic blessings
Your silk butterfly always brings?

REDEMPTION

The clock codes zero.
Fall, winter, spring, summer, blind.
Doves bless Eve's window.

HUMANE

We put down pets in pain,
But we kill each other plain.

Humane?

We covet creative cooks,
But we censor books.

Humane?

We celebrate mirth,
But we drill into the Earth.

Humane?

We shoot fireworks in July,
But we poison the sky.

Humane human:

When will we live up to the name?

NUMBED

Your breath stood at the door.
The warmongering dentist hovered,
But another worked.
Dreams, desires, discipline,
What for? We're all in the chair,
Constipated with fear.

I HOPE I'M NAKED WHEN THE BOMB GOES OFF

I hope I'm naked when the bomb goes off.
TV on and beer aplenty, a loving chair in frenzy,
The one we copulated in for days,
The one born of fantasy after the end.

When this *new* new end comes,
I want to come too, instant death
In the searing heat well past the Sahara.
Will you sing us a beautiful song?

I hope I'm naked when the bomb goes off.
Engaged with you on a red leather sofa,
Mists of ecstasy won't save us, but we
Shall display anyway—bodies pressed in joy.

After the flash, I want our silhouettes
Married to stone, wed to the wall,
Like notches on a bedpost, a moist
Spot in the midst of destruction.

I hope I'm naked when the bomb goes...

DESENSITIZED PLANK

Naked women in windowless rooms,
Another gunman, multiple deaths,
Regurgitant elephants parade
Through dark rooms blind,
We spend time, losing essence,
An assuage to reality, to carnage,
To the incompetent daily
Developments, the acid rain—we
Forget—the nuclear missiles,
Hydrogen on tap, flatulent media spats,
Circuses of bombing intent,
Distractions to invent, blessings spent.
Where are *we* in this *We the People's* mess?
We prance the desensitized plank.

SEXY MANGO

The drink caught my eye,
Colors splashed into
Sacred pulp, a purge of
Pain writ large by its
Ingredients: Mango,
Strawberries, banana,
Orange, and protein power.
Useless without your allure,
The black hair, the tight
Black shoes, the breasts
Hidden beneath a black
Sweater that dreams of
An isolated beach, where
We can run bare beyond
Fear of apocalyptic eyes.
We are the most beautiful
Creatures in this vestibule,
Portal to a smooth sojourn.
Let's tumble to the sand,
The Fates fill our sentences.

PEACOCK

He inspects the best suit,
The mirror wears it well.
She hugs the corners,
The curves, the latent
Shyness, dissipated.
Colors unfurl here,
Dances and dalliances
In the dreams of dignity.

The dandy apple dangles
In light blue regalia, no
Feather, nor fedora, but
A light blue cap rigged
To wield power rests
Upon knowledge,
Soulful sassafras.
This man needs church.

HOOFING IT IN BROOKLYN AT 2:02 A.M.

Hoofing it in Brooklyn at 2:02 a.m.
The clouds are out, the moon is not.
I don't know where I am.
The taco truck, the shuttle bus,
This sultry night of June:
It might as well be noon.
The lovers in the backseat of a
Parked car smirk as I pass.
We all know what's going down.
We don't need the pungent smoke,
Or the hurried bra pulled up.
Elsewhere, howlers fill a desolate bar
To tilt a glass even if they're broke.
The night, like me, bends into
Middle age, but I'm no sage.
Perhaps tomorrow night
I'll face a better breeze.
I'll mark the hours with fruitful ease,
Then remember her lips in case we end.
Hoofing it in Brooklyn at 2:02 a.m.

27 MILLION DEGREES[16]

Plasma and gas
These itinerant eons
Hurtle at, through,
Beside, and into
Our distant future.

Love is searing heat.
Love burns.
Love illuminates.
Love transcends.
Love is in the sun's hands.

She is our mother,
The destined particles
Of everything we know,
Of everything we learn.
We are 27 million degrees.

---

[16] The approximate temperature (°F) of the sun's core.

BLACK MARROW

In spring hearth and home,
My blood's red, my marrow's Black.
We withstand attack.

BEAUTIFUL FUNERAL (Inspired by Akira Kurosawa's *The Bad Sleep Well*)

The grift is done.
The country, come undone.
All that remains for a nation,
For a city on the Hill, for truth,
For all those that voted for
A bad man who sleeps well.
Has *he* designed a beautiful funeral?
Venereal democracy?
Sidereal hypocrisy?
We're all staring at the sun.

OLD CARS IN BLACK & WHITE

Brief flashes of light are
Reflections of time past,
Memories of things
That did not last,
Now idle beneath,
Obscured stars,
A canopy of black dust.
We long for fresh rust,
An antidote to antipodean trust.
We long for a projector's blight,
Old cars to drive us from our
Postdiluvian plight.

SISYPHUS

I am the Sisyphus of Stubbornness.
There are no walls, no borders,
No distant supernovae blocking
The door. I am my enemy.
I am the gastric ship in the
Belly of a buoyant Beast.
The hills of Rome, San Francisco,
Lisbon, they are but atoms, piled
Upon other atoms, they will be
Alluvial fans, submerged entities,
With tablets of human residue,
Latent metallic bones, rage,
Dug up centuries hence, on an
Asteroid vrooming in the Void.
And what of my soul? I will
Be on this rock, this human
Continent, a future seed,
Cultivated, grown, leached.
Crushed to nothing, I rise
To shoulder time, time and again.

SPINOZA'S GOD

If everything is God,
All the natural elements,
The patriarchal torments,
Does an entity reside in bombs?
Can we still find enmity in counting
Electric Sheep when we fall asleep?
As the Doomsday Clock beeps?

Wondrous particles,
Wondrous eyes,
Wondrous minds:
Must we contort
Into dogmatic cries?
Möbius strips as
We burn naked in the wind.

SUMMER HEAT

Telephone wires, stars, and you,
Blasphemous heat in the land of ire.

We waltz through corn, dandelion,
Lightning bolts designed for tires.

Like when we were 10, ghosts said boo.
Now Fourth of July is flush with liars.

America, snap, crackle, pop.
The soil burns eternal fires.

When the hounds of blood escape the flood,
We'll need a funeral pyre.

When we're old, in the dusk, red, white, blue?
The children of 1976, bicentennial flier.

What color is the sun, that nurtures me and you?
We are the machines, the revolutionary criers.

DETERRENCE

I have a bomb.
You have a bomb.
War persists.
What happens to
Deterrence deferred?
Same threats,
Same plans,
Same bombs,
Same origami folds.
Deter, hence.

PHAETHON

I.

We are celestial bodies colliding,
Heat, friction, magnetic pull.
I cannot escape your gravity.
I wish you'd call, and we'd fall
Into an infinity bed, water
Cascading becomes steam.

II.

You are the voice of the wind,
I am defenseless against the
Siren force exerted in the dark
Corners of dusty musical rooms.
Blow air upon our nakedness,
Scold the moon, temper the sun.

III.

I am a diamond in your hands,
Firm against the imaginative
Motion of tenderness, care,
Beauty, tranquility, dares.
We mine the thrilling depths,
We dine in the pillars of ecstasy.

IV.

I am naked before you.
I cannot hide my desire.
It's transparent glass in
Your coaxing mirror.
Let us grip the tides
Of engorgement we admire.

V.

I want to heal your broken body
With the streams of joy,
Strokes of undulating forever.
Your hips, divine, astride
Dark hair, their beckoning care.
We must worship abandon.

VI.

You are the regal star, and
I am your obedient planet.
I, too, am your volcano, your
Basalt column rising from
The magma of our exquisite
Thoughts, branded in longing.

VII.

You are your own goddess,
Bathed and noted, your
Radiant blue eyes fell gods.
I am kindle in your fire,
I exhale your name in
The pangs of pleasure.

VIII.

I am a fountain spraying fire,
Phaethon, bound by each part of you.
Touch me, wreck me, but
Please do it with thermonuclear
Precision to fuel
My lost enchantments.

WHAT IS MEMORY?

Did I ride a Big Wheel?
Or did I see a picture
Of myself riding said Big Wheel?
Which came first?
The photo or the memory egg?
The dimes or the adventures?
1970s mien and means,
We ate beans and rice,
Acted naughty or nice.
We didn't have personal screens.
We did things to elicit Polaroid screams:
Rollercoasters, dirt-clod fights,
Illegal fireworks on the
Fourth of July, remembered
Blue sky, tie dye, apple pie.
Do they linger in my synapses?
Do images preclude experience?
Don't ask me; I'm green,
Creating new energy,
New vats of mindful nudity.

What is memory?
Do I still hear its melody?

THE SALT COMES AT UNUSUAL TIMES

The salt comes at unusual times,
In and out with the tide, unbound,
Up and down with the morning sound.

We marinate together, these fluids and I,
Tended by a grateful eye, a kind
Doctor of one's own mind, unblind.

Ambivalence is not my friend,
But sadness and girth give birth to streams,
The stateliness of actionable dreams.

Words flow on the page like drops on the cheek.
I, among the meek, smile, glisten in glory.
There are no beginnings, no ends to this story.

TRAINS AT 3:39 A.M.

The night abides the rumbling hum,
Considering the broken sound of tumbling silence
That allows such Sturm und Drang.

Oil cars have the sleekest vibration,
Smooth like ice freezing in winter,
Imperceptible except to the discerning ear.

The connecting cables of their brethren
Rattle with true freedom, their cargo
Bleeds banal and suffers kingdoms.

DESERT ISLAND MOVIES

The Godfather of this *Isle of Dogs* will
Do the Right Thing to live *La Dolce Vita*, be it
The Good, the Bad and the Ugly, or a
Blade Runner-esque run to pick up
Some *Pulp Fiction* at the jetsam bookstore.

So, before the world erupts into *Star Wars*,
And *Aliens* arrive above cities,
The Man Who Fell to Earth makes
Another *Last Tango in Paris* pilgrimage.

Alas, civilization *Dr. Strangelove*'s into the
Planet of the Apes, and the world
Has but *8 ½* revolutions.

ADVERTISING

Hot values. Cool finds.
Breaking news. Free rides.

Stop the steel?
Apocalyptic man of steal.

America rising?
Advertising.

SCREAMS OF THE DEAD

What is the cure for torture?
Listen to the screams of the dead.
Play their sounds, a siren, day and night.
Their pain is our pain.
We stumble every time.

THE ARCHAIC WARD

Straw for the crazed man, straitjacket for
Another. Am I a man in an archaic ward?
Or do I just write about one, keeping myself alive in the telling?
We are all naked, Patient X.

13%

Write fast.
The empty vase
On the mantel
Disappears as
The imagination
Of the world recedes.

Become a child.
Then you will see.
You will know
What to do.
You will find
Glory in an old shoe.

THE DOG WITH ONE EYE

The dog with one eye sees more than me.
Beach vibes on a leash, cute eye, a smile.
The dogs of summer, the leisurely glutes,
Leering men in three-piece suits.
The dogs of humidity, the puffy white clouds,
The girls in their element, men on chains,
They think they're free, but no domain.
Dishes unwashed, coffee stains, the man
In the street who *Jesus* preaches.
Ice cream slicks, oil drips, pantomimes
Wave their sticks, polka dots, and linen sins,
The women waft in their affairs, men
Duck the lairs of hidden colors,
Party with disinherited "cousins," the kids on
The corner playing the dozens, this dog
Looks left, this dog looks right, unseen
Terrors nowhere in sight. Laughs, crashes,
Stocks, blockades, trips, that party
Last week, the molasses still spilled.
The dog with one eye sees more than we.

THE BIG BANGS

It went on for some time.
Supernovae in the Iowa summer night.
I was a new fiend in a new city.
Walking alone under a shifting sky.
Crackling words, crackling pity, I
Popped a pittance of pith in my paltry mind,

How could I describe the guiding might?

The darkness, of a larger kind, made light,
Commanded "look at me.
I am the horizon, your destiny.
Let me show you what you must know."

I stopped, peered above, neon Kanji
Written against the shrouded clouds,
Brief sparks of wisdom to speed read.
Each mini nuclear blast a directive,
God spoke in questions:

How many waterfalls rush this Earth?

How many lovers seek rapture in the dark?

How many stars burn beyond the booming penumbrae?

Maybe the Creator didn't know,
Correspondences that can't be answered.
Nonetheless, I divined more.

How many words will flow from the world?

How many worlds will flow from the Word?

The night preacher emitted his streaks,
Each a unique tact, taut in a tiny universe.
I remained in awe; I needed a whiskey sour to
Plug in a lightbulb. Maybe that's why she left.

The electricity shorted. The bangs ceased.

As I opened my front door,
I pondered the possibilities,
Lightning sometimes strikes thrice.

COLD DRINKS

When the sun's surprise
Debrides the dark River Styx,
Exact change only.

HOPEFUL AI LIE

Chemical, biological, and radiological arms dismantle themselves.

GIANT

I am your giant, the tallest on the plain,
The nimblest Panhandle suitor as the
Flames of apocalypse take us all.
The billboards never last.

We laugh at the bleeding clouds,
Shrug at the fungi in the grasslands,
Detour along the not-so-scenic
Radiation superhighway.

We are the mutants, the gorges
On every horizon, painted suns
Against the fabric of America.
The landscape takes our virginity.

WAKING BEFORE THE SUN

I awoke before the sun,
Crept out the vacant window
In a desert of my choosing,
Drawn by her power.
The sky mottled midnight as
I walked the Ridge of Doom,
A silhouette against the limn
Of darkness at my back,
A marionette in time.
Her glorious presence
Filled the horizon,
Nuclear fire, but
I didn't melt in this nightmare.
There were no other souls,
No dinner plates, no ice cream.
A bleak afterlife stared back.
Stark tides of confusion,
Illusion only works with
A watcher, a willing audience
Waiting for seduction.

The black soot beneath my feet
Crystallized in the overwhelming bright.
Red, yellow, and orange flames
Danced into every shape,
Every imagination's manifestation.

The sun winked; I lifted my hands,
Placed them one on each cheek,
To ensure I hadn't already departed.
These enduring seconds, this
Enduring trip without a sound.
No, I heard a faint cry as
My footsteps quickened.
The resonance kissed the blinding light.
Louder, the wail grew, but
Its provenance eluded logic.
A newborn's coos engaged the realm.
Together—the sun, the lost child, the soot,
The surreal bridge of tomorrow—
We became fast friends.
We held hands until I rose,
Confused, in the midst of heat.

MY HEROES KILLED YOUR HEROES

I saw its ilk on a bumper sticker in a movie.
South Dakota plates, numbers, dates,
Rearranged on the Great Plains.
Everyone in their tribes, everyone's groovy?
Outside, do we have to fall in line?
If the words are followed, everyone's dead,
Lamented mountains, majestic reds,
Daisies pushing up uncouth.
If there are no killers, we'll be fine.
We don't crave heroes, we crave truth.

HER NAME WAS CALLIOPE

They found her body downstream.
Dreams, reams of paper tattered,
The metal man with a detector.
His mother told him long ago:
"Find a penny pick it up, and
All day you'll have good luck."
He lifted some lyrics from a piece here,
Another there, some lost to gusts.
The man left them to another wanderer,
A cowboy with an imagination.

She was the most beautiful girl
Anyone had known, unflinched,
Unguarded, the grace of a silent auction.
She had visions of nuclear war
Not knowing she approached Helen of Troy:
Fisticuffs at bars, jukebox digressions,
Men locked in mortal combat
For no good damn reason.
No one knew what happened that night.
Now they all sing Calliope's *canción*.

THE POWER OF NO

Just don't do it:
Say no.
No to nuclear weapons.
No to authoritarianism.
No to censorship.
No to gerrymandering.
No to the Electoral College.
No to tax incentives for the rich.
No to recidivism.
No to sour cream in prison.
No to ignorant clowns.
No to racism.
No to poisoning Earth.
No to the Confederate flag.
No to Capitol rotunda rioters.
No to convicted felons in the Oval.
No to broken umbrellas.
No to mendacious flies.
No to war.
No to poverty.
No to famine.
No to homogeneity.
No to building more bombs.
No to immigrants must go.
Say *yes* to saying no.

PURPOSE

The itinerant man looks for new lands,
Not to conquer, to savor, absorb, learn,
To replenish the future, destine the children.
Those left behind, drip like cursive,
Can any among the despondent read?
Or do tricks at the circus pass for need?
The travelers know, they have purpose,
They cradle the world, create destinations.
They'll inherit the Earth, know no foreign coast.
For every hanging grape is home, not a boast.

VEXILLA REGIS PRODEUNT INFERNI

Democracy dies on a downward escalator in daylight.

ROD SERLING NARRATES A NUCLEAR WAR

A brazen man and the big, tall wish,
Fortified by military stripes,
Weaponry of the most
Modern kind, and the
Grit of a small child
Who wanted to be
A fighter pilot way
Back when. Today,
Child Abel will kill
All of us, Cain,
When he enters a
Code, talks into
A red phone. His
Boyhood wishes guide us
Into the gray area,
Not magical,
Where bombs can
Lead to another world,
Where peace and
Strange physics mix,
Where words and just laws
Remain fixed,
A world we call...

BIKINIS AT THE END OF THE WORLD

Operation Crossroads[17]:
July 1946, Bikini Atoll:

Let's commence,
There is no recompense.

Test Able[18].
Test Baker[19].
Point A to Point B of destruction.
Peel back the onion.

A peaceful day,
The clouds played
"Ring Around The Rosie,"
Prelude to Black Death.
Rosie is not a pretty girl,
Her ring is a 20th-century rash.
Her pocket full of posies...
Let's not smell this scourge.
Mushroom murk doesn't
Play well with others.

---

[17] A pair of nuclear tests at Bikini Atoll in July 1946; the first conducted in the Pacific's Marshall Islands.
[18] An airburst nuclear detonation 520 feet above Bikini Atoll on July 1, 1946.
[19] An underwater nuclear blast in Bikini Lagoon on July 25, 1946, that caused more destruction than test Able.

Imagery, imagery, imagery.
Détente. Imaginary peace.

Invited scientists,
Honored guests.
What about the Bikinians[20]?
They still can't return
To their lagoon in 2025.
They don't punctuate
Their history with
Christmas trees,
With fascist red signs.
They look at their lagoon
On the evening news,
Egos bruised, mustn't
Display that. Let's push
Other buttons,
Something sexist.
Can we promote
Authoritarianism
With a two-piece?
Fool the masses
With pressed flesh?

---

[20] In winter 1946, the U.S. Navy moved the 167 people living on Bikini Atoll to the much smaller Rongerik Atoll, which the Bikinians believed was haunted by malevolent spirits. Bikinians were again moved—to Kwajalein Atoll—in 1948; then soon after to Kili Atoll (some later chose to live on Jaluit Atoll) until eventually in 1972, three families repatriated Bikini. However, when many Bikinians had Cesium-137 levels well beyond body limits, they were moved to Ejit Island on Majuro Atoll. They still have not been able to return. (Source: The Marshall Islands Program).

The civilized are never
Forced to march.
They adjudicate who to deport.
You were here first? No more.
They contain the masses' disdain.
What happens beneath
A common moon when
Sea levels submerge the brain?
We'll find a new
Proving ground.

Let's create fresh snow,
Origami in a flash.
Hiroshima? Nagasaki?
Less than 12 months later,
We needed new clothes.
New targets, new distractions.
Vixens and bombshells
Stirred fashion on a white sand beach.
Today, we call them tourists,
United by the heat
Of the sun, a dark
Commotion of riches,
Priorities in disarray.
National guard deployed
While the world sunbathes.
Instituted by a piece of cloth
(or none at all), instruments
Of 21st century distraction,
1950s mien until the end of the world,
Strings that men have pulled.

Such a cultural polka-dotted weapon,
We still call it a bikini.
Take a name along with ancestors' land.
Itsy-bitsy for small hands,
Garage bands, cheap
Corvette gas, teeny weenies,
Constitutional lapses.

Hey ho, whaddya know?

Revel in Bikini nomenclature.
What bombs will we make next?
They won't increase our stature.
The scientists, the lost,
Citizens of Earth,
What happened?
We dropped *two* bombs,
And yet, we seek new
Death rays, ocean sprays,
Tariffs, what's mine is mine,
And what's yours is mined too.
We don't meet at
The Crossroads. We sell lies.
In Times Square, we
Drop the ball and stare.
New Year, new scares.
Pandora's wind is already had.
We're well past midnight now.
Grey is the new pastel.

Ashes, ashes, we all fall down.

EDEN

Is rainwater in a silver cup,
A pot, clean animal meat,
A can opener, air-conditioning,
Birds at the windowsill,
Entertainment, electricity
Streamed like air, cars
With pollution undeterred,
A vegetable garden, grown
In perfection; books, medicine,
Cellphones with inane games,
Communication, magic, shelter,
Jackrabbits on a spit, matches,
Infinite lighter fluid, infinite
Things with no cost like rocks,
Canned food without radiation,
Hospital care, doctors on call,
Healthy food on demand, fast food
On command, a bastard child
Cared and adorned, a blizzard
Borne in a winter's coat,
Heat in the Nordic ice,
Catamarans, satellites,
Computers, condoms,
Bodegas at 3:33 a.m.,
Mathematics, salt, butter,
Sane neighbors without guns,

Bonfires from the banister,
To melt every cold heart.
Eden is.... the
Realization it will end.

OBOETE (覚えて, REMEMBER)

Before I levitate, my love, I leave you with these.
Remember them well.

Water is cold.
People should not be.

Chew with your mouth closed.
No one will know what you're eating.

Endless desire leads to endless laziness.
Want nothing, achieve it all.

The winter child dreams of summer.
The summer child lives in summer.

A is just another letter.
Z savors every breath.

Summer clouds bring much needed rain.
Mushroom clouds are showoffs.

Make love before you die.
Make hate disappear at birth.

The rock in the river never quits.
It just changes with time.

Summer colds should remind you of winter's breath.
Winter colds should remind you of summer's breeze.

If your eyes are closed, you should be asleep.
If your eyes are open, you should be fulfilling dreams.

Go to the ends of the Earth,
But not the end of the story.
The ends of the earth instruct Earth will end.
The end is the *end*.

SETSUKO[21]

Leaders: Listen.
Listen to the
Still beating hearts.

Listen to Setsuko.
Hear her.
Love her.
Respect her.

Follow her lead.
She seeks peace.
She speaks peace.

Remember all the others.
Their names,
Their faces,
Their places.

Hibakusha[22].

---

[21] Thirteen-year-old Setsuko Thurlow (née Nakamura) survived the atomic blast at Hiroshima and is a world-renowned activist for the abolition of nuclear weapons. A leading voice of the International Campaign to Abolish Nuclear Weapons (ICAN), she gave the acceptance speech when the organization was awarded a Nobel Peace Prize in 2017.

[22] Survivors of the nuclear blasts in Hiroshima and Nagasaki on Aug. 6 and Aug. 9, 1945.

Listen to their stories.
Lest we all disappear.

Flesh

Hanging

From

Bones.

Eyeballs held in hands.

Moruroa, Ekker, Semipalatinsk, Maralinga, Fangataufa, Bikini[23].

Listen...

Fill the Earth with hope.
Kill insanity.

---

[23] Places across the globe that have been the site of nuclear testing.

NUCLEAR NON-PROLIFERATION ORGANIZATIONS

For more information on what you can do to help abolish, as well as prevent the use and spread of nuclear weapons, here is a list of some prominent nuclear non-proliferation organizations. This list is in alphabetical order and by no means comprehensive; however, we all hold the power to act.

Abolition 2000: https://www.abolition2000.org

Alliance for Nuclear Accountability: https://www.ananuclear.org

Arms Control Center: https://armscontrolcenter.org/about/

Beyond Nuclear: https://beyondnuclear.org

Bulletin of the Atomic Scientists: https://thebulletin.org/

Campaign for Nuclear Disarmament: https://cnduk.org/

Global Zero: https://www.globalzero.org/

Greenpeace:
https://www.greenpeace.org/usa/climate/issues/nuclear/

International Campaign to Abolish Nuclear Weapons (ICAN):
https://www.icanw.org/

International Committee of the Red Cross:
https://www.icrc.org/en/law-and-policy/nuclear-weapons

International Physicians for the Prevention of Nuclear War:
https://www.ippnw.org/

James Martin Center for Nonproliferation Studies:
https://nonproliferation.org

Mayors for Peace:
https://www.mayorsforpeace.org

Nuclear Age Peace Foundation:
https://www.wagingpeace.org

Nuclear Information and Resource Service (NIRS):
https://www.nirs.org

Nuclear Threat Initiative:
https://www.nti.org/

Parliamentarians for Nuclear Non-Proliferation and Disarmament (PNND):
https://www.pnnd.org

Peace Action:
https://www.peaceaction.org/what-we-do/campaigns/world-without-nuclear-weapons/

Pugwash Conferences on Science and World Affairs:
https://pugwash.org

Reaching Critical Will:
https://www.reachingcriticalwill.org

United Nations Office for Disarmament Affairs:
https://disarmament.unoda.org/wmd/nuclear/npt/
https://disarmament.unoda.org/wmd/nuclear/tpnw/

Physicians for Social Responsibility:
https://psr.org/

Vienna Center for Disarmament and Non-Proliferation (VCDNP):
https://vcdnp.org

ACKNOWLEDGMENTS

First and foremost, thank you to my family, my wife and daughters. Thank you, Mom and Dad (R.I.P.), and my brothers. And thank you to many, many others: The Bias Family, The Pitts Family, The Takahashi Family, The Tanaka Family, The Lao Arpasuwong Family, our Brooklyn friends and neighbors, The Cervantes Family; The Sigur Family and everyone on Light Street; Faisal Azam and Brian Jaramillo, who were particularly helpful in editing the collection; professor Margaret Ross and everyone in the July 2025 poetry workshop at the Iowa Writers' Workshop; Samiya Bashir, *Cave Canem*, and everyone in the fall 2025 *Cave Canem* NYC regional workshop; Lisa P. LeGrand, Andrew Paredes and Family, Jamille McClendon, Robson Garcia, Chilembwe Mason; James Chan, Hiromi Saeki, Chi Mac, Erica Velis, John Plenge, Anne Vallersnes, Paul Gutierrez, Dimitry Léger, Naomi Castillo, Lisa Darling, Karen Lee, Caryn Prime, Scott Hevesy, Jaramay Aref, Richard Demak, Larry Mondi, Joy Birdsong, Natasha Simon, Susan Szeliga, Diane Smith, Gabe Miller, Sonja Kiefer, Bettina Meetz, João Serejo, Kevin Gidden, Dave Weiss (and everyone from Disneyland), Karen Strauss, Cynthia Cortes, Jennymar, Mrs. Pell, Bob Der, Mike Johnson, Julian Rozzell Jr., and the cast and crew of all my independent films; Seevon Chau and family, Marina and Jason Anderson of Polgarus Studio, David Gendelman, John Banta, Brendan Barr, and everyone at *Vanity Fair*; everyone at St. Matthias, Willie Joe Philbin and The Philbin Family; my friends, fraternity brothers, and football teammates at the University of Arizona; my classmates at NYU; as well as everyone I have encountered throughout life. I learn from you all and marinate in gratitude.

Kelvin C. Bias

New York City, Sept. 2025

OTHER WORK BY KELVIN C. BIAS

MILKMAN (Novel)

What happens when everyman Calder Boyd starts to lactate? The Manhattanite becomes a media cause célèbre nicknamed the Milkman and old and new problems spill forth. The son of a former NBA star and a Norwegian artist, Calder copes with his strained marriage, losing his copywriting job at a boutique ad agency, a male-empowerment espousing mailman and a porn-star performance artist who wants to exploit him. He also deals with his late father's legacy and his wife's past indiscretion—all while breastfeeding their newborn daughter. Calder eventually becomes a pawn in the battle between a feminist organization and a militant men's society as he tries to become a better husband and man. The Fourth Estate, sex, art, love, memory, marriage and family converge during the snowiest winter on record in this commentary on contemporary American fatherhood.

WHISPERS OF A DYING SUN (Poetry)

These poems represent the vestiges of man from the perspective of a distant future. Akin to radio signals, the remnants of humanity streak toward a black hole where art, politics, love, technology, philosophy, science and the yearning for eternity accrete. Prophetic, stoic, polyphasic, the words disassemble and recombine on the other side in search of a new sun. I hope these poems find a closer home in your personal universe, heard but you're unsure of their origin, like whispers.

SEXOPOLIS: POEMS ON LOVE AND SEX

Love is a liberation, an act, a rebellion, a restriction, a communion. This poetry collection covers the universal topics of love and sex. From erotic to platonic and from marital to familial, love comes in many forms. We don't always get it, but we all crave it.

IMMACULATE DUST: LOVE POEMS

This poetry collection delves headlong into the world of love. Encompassing the realms of dream, fantasy and reality, the poems intend to engender not just love, but more pointedly, lovemaking. Lust. Love. Languor. These are three states of mind and body before, during and after the most pleasant poetry of human interaction: consented sex. We all possess desire, and we are all made of dust. Immaculate dust.

21 PARTICLES OF ETERNITY (Poetry)

Is eternity a quantifiable entity? An existence that can be divided into smaller particles, assembled and disassembled like a puzzle? Can it be bent? Borrowed? Recycled? Eternity is elusive. It constantly seems beyond our grasp yet always within our reach. *21 Particles of Eternity* covers topics as disparate as Mars and pornography and ranging from global warming and parenthood to politics and death. The poet posits this: perhaps there are hidden portals where eternity can be glimpsed for fleeting moments, and the quest to find them brings meaning. How many particles will you find?

IF THE SKY IS AWAKE (Poetry)

Why do we have a 24-hour day, 60-minute hour, and 60-second minute? Thank the ancient Egyptians, Sumerians and Babylonians. Going further back, in humanity's early days, time was simply measured by the interval between sunrise and sunset. Today, we have much more precise methods. One second is defined as the duration of 9,192,631,770 periods of the radiation corresponding to the transition between the two hyperfine levels of the ground state of a cesium 133 atom. Confusing? Yes. Sometimes what transpires in daylight is the purest. Each day is a new dawn, a chance to reinvent yourself, find new love, rekindle an old one, and peer into the sky and feel awake. Reading poetry is like living life by your own clock. Lose yourself in your own sky.

THE LAST WILL & TESTAMENT OF THE UNITED STATES OF AMERICA: POETRY

This poetry collection conveys my anger and sadness over the current state of America—black, brown, yellow, red, white, and blue. On May 25, 2020—Memorial Day—a white woman named Amy Cooper walked her dog without a required leash in an area of Central Park known as the Ramble, and Christian Cooper, a peaceful, bird-watching black man, asked her to leash her dog.

The legacy of slavery writ-large in the astounding fact they had the same surname. Amy responded by calling 911 to say that "an African American man" was threatening her and her dog. Christian calmly recorded the incident. (Imagine what might have happened if he hadn't.) The video went viral and provided a painful reminder of the tradition of white women falsely accusing black men of a crime. Later that night, in Minneapolis, Minnesota, a black man named George Floyd, who was not resisting arrest, was pressed face down into the pavement with a knee to his neck for nine minutes—*nine* minutes—by white Minneapolis police officer Derek Chauvin. Floyd died as he narrated his own death. "I can't breathe." Protests over Floyd's killing raged in cities across America for days, weeks...forever? On July 17, John Lewis, civil rights icon and Georgia Congressman, died from pancreatic cancer, and a few days before he passed, he wrote an essay to be released on the day of his funeral. On July 30, it ran in *The New York Times*. In his essay, Lewis wrote: "When you see something that is not right, you must say something. You must do something." *The Last Will & Testament of the United States of America* is the poet's way of saying and doing "something."

L.: POEMS

On May 13, 2020, I turned 50 years old. It was just another day. Just another day of worrying about my family, worrying about the state of the world, worrying about finding a job, worrying about COVID-19, and tantrums, and remote learning, wondering what I would do for the next 50 years, *if* I lived that long. To celebrate turning 50, to celebrate existence in general, I decided to write a poem for every year of my life. The process made me wonder:

What have I truly accomplished in 50 years? Which begged another question. Is it important?

BLUE MILK: POEMS

Blue Milk is a mood: A concoction of poetry for your collection. The eighth book of poems by Kelvin C. Bias emerges from the idea of creating personal libations—with actual liquids or metaphorical ones. A drink may start with something as simple as a glass of milk, and end with something profound far beyond our blue planet. The choice is yours.

LIFEBLOOD (Poetry)

Love is the lifeblood of humanity. Enter this portal to desire, dreams, and destiny: a little red book.

THE LAST WILL & TESTAMENT OF THE UNITED STATES OF AMERICA: CODICIL EDITION

Poet Kelvin C. Bias adds 17 poems—indicting the Jan. 6 insurrection, mass shootings, and the rise of American fascism—in this Codicil version of the 2020 WILL of the United States of America.

IF YOU COULD BE EVERY COLOR (Poetry)

Aren't we more than just the visible spectrum of light? Our human eyes can detect wavelengths from 380 to 700 nanometers. What if we could see everything—below and beyond that range? What would we discover, about the universe and about ourselves? What will you uncover in *If You Could Be Every Color*?

NUDE BLUE (Poetry)

The word "blue" holds several meanings: the color, melancholy, learned, intellectual, Puritanical, profane, risqué, the sea, the sky, a Union soldier in the American Civil War, exasperated (blue in the face), unexpectedly (out of the blue), and even political affiliation. This naked collection of provocative poems encompasses blue in various shades.

DARLING: Poems

These poems embody thoughts whispered to your darling: confessions, dreams, desires, memories, fantasies—as if prying into a secret diary.

FEEDING GRAPES TO THE GODDESS: Poems

Feeding grapes to royalty is an ancient idea. Whether this is historically accurate is up for debate, nevertheless, anyone can partake. This collection of love poems hopes to stimulate such passionate action. Whom do you want to indulge?

WE DREAM HERE: Poems

Home is childhood, and childhood is home. Where you grew up, be it one place or many, and where you first dreamed, are places we often return to in adulthood. WE DREAM HERE is an aspiration and a philosophy.

ANGEL OF LOVE (Poetry)

Everyone needs a muse. Even muses. In this collection of love poems, everyone's a muse: jazz singers, suitors, old men, older women, antiquarians, insomniacs, masseuses, Vegas gamblers, and bygone Hollywood starlets. Who is your Angel of Love?

PLEASURE: Poems

Pleasure skirts danger. The word bleeds from the tongue, bent to the ends of individual persuasion, and as such, great thinkers have planted their insignia on its promise and peril. For example, French philosopher Voltaire wrote that "illusion is the first of all pleasures." Early 19th century English author Jane Austen said, "one half of the world cannot understand the pleasures of the other." Perhaps the Stoic statesman Seneca provides the most useful perspective: "Enjoy present pleasures in such a way as not to injure future ones." From the innocent to the seductive, from the epicurean to the carnal, enjoy this pleasureful poetry collection.

ABOUT THE AUTHOR

Kelvin C. Bias is a journalist, novelist, poet, filmmaker, and raconteur. However, his most important designation is father. He holds a B.A. in Political Science from the University of Arizona and an M.F.A in Screenwriting from NYU. He lives in New York City with his family.

www.ingramcontent.com/pod-product-compliance
Lightning Source LLC
Chambersburg PA
CBHW050905160426
43194CB00011B/2296